The Vocation of Management

Julia J. Underwood, Ph.D.
Professor of Management
Azusa Pacific University

Ruth Anna Abigail, Ph.D.
Professor Emeritus
Azusa Pacific University

The Vocation of Management

ISBN-13: 978-1519481306

ISBN-10: 1519481306

Dedication

We dedicate this book to all the students who have enriched our lives as we shared learning experiences in the classroom. You are the reason we teach, and you are the reason we have written this text.

.

Table of Contents

Foreword

Though we have not met, and are not likely to meet face to face until we are gathered to His side, still, at this point in time, God has placed me in your life, and you in mine. Why God should do so, I do not understand, but today, on this day, I shall set aside my doubts and listen to that "voice" that speaks deeply from within the core of my being.

I am a Professor of Psychology and a retired licensed clinical psychologist. For over forty years now, I have taught at the college and university level, though always at a secular institution.

I was born and raised in what was then the relatively small agri-business town of Fresno, located in the Central Valley of California. It was in 1958, when I was but eleven years old, that Billy Graham brought his crusade to Fresno. My childhood friend, Terry, and I got on our bikes and rode the two or three miles to the stadium where the crusade would be held. We sat on the highest row in the stadium, but when the call to Christ came, we both walked down those steps and onto the football field to accept Christ as our Lord and Savior.

Though God knew I was to be called into being before time itself was established, and I have always been God's, I mark that day as the first day of my walk with Him. It is a walk that continues to this day, though on a brambled path with twists and turns, and most certainly with too many stumbles and falls, often of my own making. Too often, I turned away from God, choosing my way over Him. Never did that work out well for long. Always, God remained faced towards me. Always God called me back to him. Always God trusted me to return.

While you will know the authors of this book, The Vocation of Management, as Professor Julia Underwood, Ph.D. and Professor Ruth Anna Abigail, Ph.D., I, due to my age and perhaps our shared professional standing, know them as simply Julia and Ruth Anna. I say this because it was just a few months ago that I was sent a draft of this book to examine along with the request that I consider writing the fore-piece you are reading now. Julia thought I was the person who could and should do this. I doubted her wisdom, but out of respect, I sat down and began to read. We were to meet for dinner that night, and upon completing my first reading of the text, I wrote a hurried email:

Julia and Ruth Anna:

I do so look forward to being with you this evening. I find myself writing in the margins of the draft you sent me, even though I have four chapters to prep and two examinations to write. Know that the voice with which you write will not permit a fast read, for as is your intent, your words trigger thought. For years, I have said to myself, others, and my clients, when permitted, "God calls each of us to a place and way of being in the world."

For your students, the "place" of being, at least at this point in time, is business management; the way of being is as a child of His creation. While the first is open to change, the second is not, and since it is not, it is a child of His creation that they are to find the ground of their being.

If you think of your text as a prayer that you have for your students, namely that they ground their vocation in Christ's call from the cross, your text calls for a benediction at the end.

Here is what comes to mind, and then I must do my work:

"In the beginning was the Word, and the Word was made flesh. God spoke each of you into being and has called each of you to a place and way of being in this world. Wherever you go, wherever you are, there also

> is He. Listen for God's presence in all that
> you say, all that you do, all that you are, and
> from that place, and that place alone, fulfill
> and find fulfillment in your calling to
> vocation."~B.

I have reread the manuscript given to me several times now, and I have not changed my sense of what Professors Underwood and Abigail have provided you in the text that follows.

The next time you are in class, look to your left and to your right. These are your fellow nestlings. Today you share food and thoughts. Tomorrow, or soon after, you will stand on the edge of your nest, flap your wings, and make your descent into the world. You will be scattered, separated, perhaps never to meet again this side of the veil, but as you go, you will take a part of your fellow nestlings with you precisely because you were permitted to commune at this time and in this place graced by His love.

It is a privilege to be in community. I have just returned from my fifty-year high school reunion. At first, it was difficult to recognize one another, but then, through the wrinkles, especially when you looked into their eyes my fellow nestlings re-emerged and again we were of the nest. Today you share your dreams, as I just recently shared my memories.

When I taught at the University, as my students would sit for their final examination in a lecture hall that seated four-hundred, I would, in my mind's eye, sing a benediction over them, unbeknownst to them, that our Lord would bless them and keep them and make His face shine upon them.

I was not permitted to pray with my students nor over my students, for the ground upon which we met was claimed by the secular. But this is not the case for you. Though you may think that you are simply in your seat in a classroom, you meet on sacred ground. You meet in a consecrated place claimed by Christ. Though it may appear to you are in a classroom, you are in a sanctuary, and though you may think the person next to you is a classmate, they are a part of the congregation to which you belong and to the congregation granted you by His grace and His grace alone.

In the text provided you by Professors Underwood and Abigail, you are invited to use the lens of your faith and grounding in Christ to place the constructs of the fundamentals of business management in perspective using what is called the "dialogical approach." You will be called upon to examine, draw upon, and share your reflections as to how it is that your calling by Christ to vocation affects and informs all you say and do in a world that all too often feels dominated by that which is simply secular.

Professors Underwood and Abigail will provide you with no answers to the questions they ask, nor to the questions you will ask of yourself and your fellow students/congregants. They are simply fellow pilgrims making their own progress in this world. They will, however, provide food for thought and exercises to initiate and stimulate your thoughts. For example, you will be asked, "How can you speak truth into situations unless you have a firm grasp on what truth is in that situation as it applies to God's word, and your responsibility in that." For each of the four fundamentals of business management: planning, controlling, organizing, and leading, Professors Underwood and Abigail will ask, and ask again, how and where your grounding in Christ will inform what it is that you will choose to do as a business manager. You will be asked to move from the secular to the holy and back again time and time again until within yourself, you will find that the secular can become simply the expression of the holy, and that sound business management and actions generated on the basis of a deep and abiding faith are not only compatible, one (sound business management) necessarily follows from actions based on the other (a grounding in one's faith.)

Vocation, Professors Underwood and Abigail

remind us, is what we do in response to being called to the Cross. While vocation may change, Christ's call remains eternal. Thus, each of us, called by Christ, shall, each day, this side of veil, find our ultimate grounding when we respond to our vocation through the lens of our faith.

At one point, Professors Underwood and Abigail poignantly cite the work of J. Fowler (2000) in which Fowler identifies fundamental "gifts" that embracing our occupation gives us and offers to us. Summarizing Fowler's contribution to understanding vocation, Professors Underwood and Abigail write, "Our lives are not segmented pieces but whole experiences that lead us to joyous reunion with our Creator when our Creator calls us home." When speaking of planning, Professors Underwood and Abigail suggest to us that sound business management planning grounds itself on the principles of humility, justice, and mercy. Again and again, you will be permitted to embrace rather than set aside the fundamentals of your faith as you become adept as using the dialogical approach to formulate an understanding of the basic principles of sound business management.

It has been over twenty-five years since I was permitted to sit in Professor Ray Anderson's class on the German theologian Dietrich Bonhoeffer due to the fact that my spouse was completing her Ph.D. in clinical psychology at the School of Psychology embedded in Fuller Theological Seminary.

In his classic work, *Life Together*, written during Bonhoeffer's time in Zingst and Finkenwalde in the 1930's, Bonhoeffer wrote that it is a privilege to gather in a community of believers, a privilege granted by God's grace and God's grace alone, and that this privilege is not to be taken for granted. This is a privilege God, by his grace and His grace alone, has granted to you at this time and in this place.

As he began his book, Bonhoeffer wrote, "Behold, how good and how pleasant it is for brethren to dwell together in unity!" (citing Ps. 133:1). Later he writes, "It is not simply to be taken for granted that the Christian has the privilege of living among other Christians. Jesus Christ lived in the midst of his enemies. At the end all his disciples deserted him. On the Cross he was utterly alone." Bonhoeffer goes on to speak of how it is that we see and find Christ in one another. Later still, he writes, "It is true, of course, that what is an unspeakable gift of God for the lonely individual is easily disregarded and trodden under foot by those who have the gifts every day. It is easily forgotten that the fellowship of Christian brethren is a gift of grace, a gift of the Kingdom of God that can any day be taken from us, that the time that still separates us from utter loneliness may be brief indeed. Therefore, let him who until now has the privilege of living a common Christian life with other Christians praise God on his knees and declare: It is grace, nothing but grace that we are allowed to live in community with Christian brethren."

Each Saturday, at 6:30 a.m., I meet with the same group of men I have met with for the past twenty-five years now. We open in prayer, study the word of God, share our lives, find Christ in one another, recognize our need for Him in each breath we take, close in prayer, and return to our individual lives. What you have been invited to do by Professors Underwood and Abigail, we, the men in my group, invite one another to do. None of us have it right yet. None of us have perfected our walk with Christ. None of us has stopped stumbling. All of us, however, have accepted Christ's claim on our being. That is why we keep coming back to sit with one another.

Professors Underwood and Abigail have invited you to draw upon the community of fellow Christians with whom you now find yourself to ground your vocation in Christ. I invite you to accept their invitation. You are nestlings now, but soon you will be asked to fly. But that is fine, because you are promised:

"...those who hope[1] in the LORD will renew their strength.[2] They will soar on wings like eagles;[3] they will run and not grow weary, they will walk and not be faint" (Isaiah 40:31, NIV).

I leave you with some lyrics I once wrote:

"Make your life a prayer. Make it a way of living. Fill your life with forgiving grace and loving sacrifice. Make your life a prayer."

This is what Professors Underwood and Abigail ask for you.

By His Grace,

Robert W. Byde, Ph.D.
Professor of Psychology
Fullerton College

The next page has room for you to make notes about your class discussion regarding Byde's foreword to this book.

Discussion Takeaways
What did you learn from your peers?

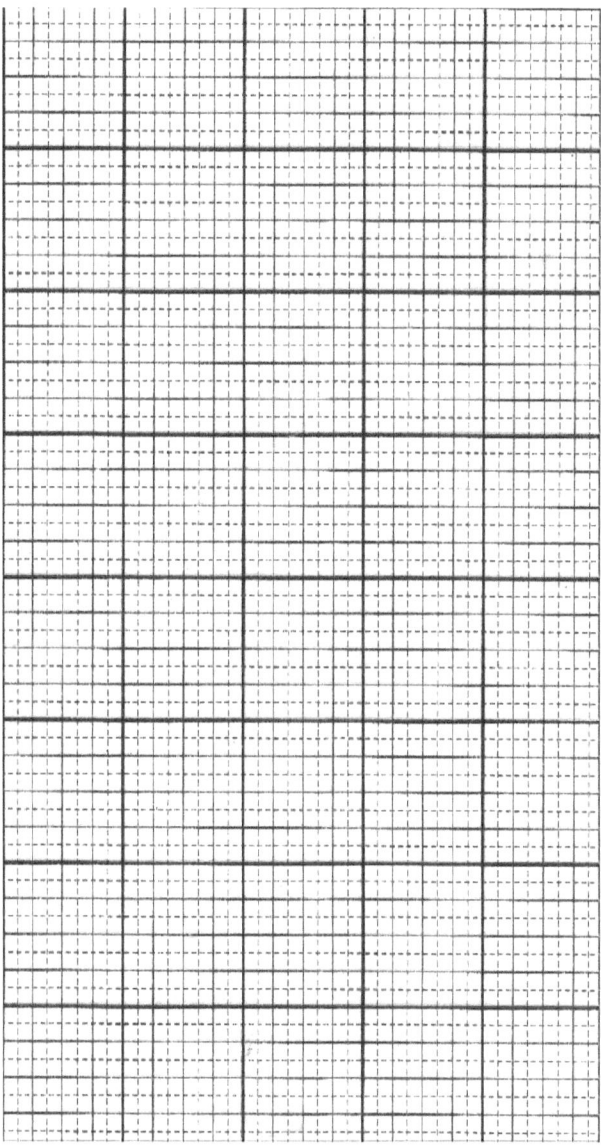

Underwood & Abigail

Introduction

<u>Purpose of the Book</u>

This text is ultimately intended for freshman and sophomore business students enrolled at faith-based institutions. Our book uses the dialogical approach described below and makes relevant the meaning of management theories in light of biblical teachings. Our intent in this book is to provide opportunities for reflection and engagement within the context of the BUSI 210—Principles of Management course at Azusa Pacific University. We want you to use this book as a means to contemplate the course material while considering big questions in life, faith perspectives, individual theology, and other's perspectives over a period of time.

Throughout the term, you will explore the principles of organization and management. As you are taking this class at a Christian institution, these theories and concepts will be contemplated in light of the Christian faith. In other words, the Bible and relevant readings about the Bible, such as biblical commentaries, will be the "lens" through which we learn about management and organization. The method we'll be using for connecting management and biblical teaching is called the "dialogical approach". This approach puts you-the student-at the center, and allows you to make connections between the bible and academic theories in a relevant way.

The Dialogical Approach

So what is the "dialogical approach?" The dialogical approach turns the learning of faith and academics "upside down". While existing methods of faith integration use biblical text to "seek" connection with discipline specific knowledge, the dialogical approach is more of a convergence of the two through dialogue and contemplation. This approach puts you at the center, and allows you to make connections between the bible and academic theories in a relevant way. In other words, rather than being told how management and faith intersect and integrate, the dialogical approach invites you to discover that integration yourself. The process for the dialogical approach includes several steps:

- Introduction of the biblical passage to be explored

- Reading of the relevant materials prior to dialogue (including complementary biblical passages, commentaries, and noted works relating to the passage)

- Exploration of cultural context of the passage

- Small and large group discussions surrounding the theological topic

- Dialogue in a creative learning process with other participants to construct shared meaning that develops as a result of the preparation and dialogue

- Assess personal meaning and application for the new learning that has resulted from the reading, one's personal experiences, the shared meaning, and creativity in the process

- Engage in on-going academic and creative work as a result of the shared learning experience

You may be asking why it is so important to understand your major from a Christian perspective. That is a very good question. In APU's purpose as a faith-based school, we expect that part of the educational experience focuses on understanding your discipline in light of Christian faith and heritage. The dialogical approach allows you to understand and apply the way that management and leadership are intricately connected with God's master plan for you to live a life of faith in the business world.

As Christians, we believe that God is the Creator, and is all knowing, and perfect. So, let's start with the Creator part of God's identity. God created the earth, animals, people, etc. However, we fail to recognize that God created our disciplines, too! Therefore, in order to really, truly understand management and leadership in a way that allows you to be the best version of a manager and leader in the future, you must first understand how God's truth speaks into these disciplines. How does God intend for managers and leaders to work in a fallen society in a way that is redemptive, above reproach (ethical), and sustainable?

So now, you may be asking why you should invest time in understanding scripture when all you really want is to pass the class and move onto other classes, graduation, and the start of your "real life." To answer that, we need to tell you a little about ourselves. Both of us went to secular universities. Our initial exposure to faith integration came as we first began teaching at APU. When we look back at our own university experiences, we see empty spaces where faith could have enhanced our understanding of our majors—and the purpose for our lives. Those empty spaces sometimes made it difficult to understand material. Sometimes we were less than enthusiastic about what we were learning because we simply did not see the point of it. Most importantly, we did not have something that helped everything "hang together"—we often felt as though we were trying to complete jigsaw puzzles without the actual picture to guide us.

Moreover, there is so much to learn in your university career! For each class, you probably get a little nervous looking at all the material and wondering how you will remember it. We believe that by associating a Christian perspective on management, it will provide you the opportunity to create a place to associate, recall and remember the concepts from the class. One of the functions of the dialogical process is that it allows you to experience the material in a "different way," a way that associates the concepts with things you have already learned outside of management.

A last question that might occur to you is how learning the connection between your discipline and Christian heritage and tradition influences your faith walk. Often when we read scriptures, we take a specific passage and apply it to specific situations as we see fit, essentially "proof texting" the scriptures. By starting with a biblical passage, and unfolding the meaning of it more thoroughly through commentaries and other biblically and theologically informed readings, we gain a much broader and deeper understanding of its meaning. The dialogical approach permits you to navigate your place in

God's world more decisively by using God's word to guide your interpretation of the bible as it relates to work. Further, this guidance is informed not only by the Word, but also by experts who have studied and written about it, in conjunction with the larger questions in life that are sought to be answered.

Asking the Big Questions: The Dialogical Approach in Action

What are the big questions that you see in our world?

- In your life?

- In industry?

- In your community?

- In society?

- In your academic discipline?

It is valuable to think of the questions that exist in our world, and more specifically, for you to identify the ones that YOU see, experience, sense, and know. Take some time and think about what the questions of life are within these five categories and jot them down. As we were each created uniquely, yet all in God's image, these big questions are a part of our soul that seeks and yearns for the answers to life's questions. So often, we have big plans: we know what WE want, we know what WE need, WE know what WE were created to do in God's design, yet seldom do we reflect on the context and environment within which we exist. Let me pose this another way: As a manager, how can you effectively resolve conflict within your direct reports unless you know what the problem is? How can you speak truth into situations unless you have a firm grasp on what truth is in that situation as it applies to God's word, and your responsibility in that?

In contemplating your responsibility, it is imperative that you have a grasp of who you are, what your values are, and what truth you operate from as your center-the core of your being. Let Julia share an analogy with you.

> *I knew someone who viewed their wardrobe as a distinct impression of their identity. She would meticulously comb through magazines, carefully assessing what others wore. This wasn't done as a means of judging others or comparing others to herself, but rather as a way of critically reflecting on who she was, determining the timeless pieces that would help build a lasting wardrobe, and comparing trends from past, present and current genres.*
>
> *I, on the other hand, was always wanting~ needing~something that a girlfriend had, or I*

had seen in a shop window, or that I thought would be "the" trendy item which would make others know how current I was with the fashion of the day. I wasn't terribly concerned with the quality of the clothing and accessories: I just wanted to fit in like every other teenage girl. However, I used those formative years trying to look like "someone" instead of building a framework that would help me reflect my true self to others.

Recently, I came across some of that person's things: a dress coat, a watch, some furnishings and several of those old magazines. As I reflected on those pieces and flipped through one of the magazines, I saw that each item was timeless—timeless in the way that the classic nature of each item transcended fashion. I then peered into my own box of high school memorabilia: and believe me, though it was fashionable at the time, I would not be caught on the street wearing some of those items today!

You, at this moment in time, are at a similar crossroad. Moreover, we are asking that you be in the moment. We are asking that you be present: present for your college experience, present for class (both physically and mentally), and present for what God will be speaking to you.

The "wardrobe" you are contemplating is the wardrobe of your mind. Who and what will you allow to form your understanding of knowledge? Co-curricular activities? Family? Friends? Books you read? How much influence should social media or video games have? During the next few years, you will be inundated with learning new things: theories, relationships, culture, etiquette, faith and your destiny. That is an overwhelming thought!

Instead of panicking about where to shove all this stuff in your brain, let us take another approach. Let us carefully plan out the ultimate goal: how to equip you for the vocation that God has called you to embrace.

So, let's be intentional about contemplating, processing, and selecting not only what we think on but also how we store it in our minds perceptually. You can choose to attend classes, read textbooks, work on group projects and "learn" the material: and you can choose what you wish to apply to your life vocationally. In addition, these conversational and reflective practices will bolster your intellectual capacity for the future. You can also choose to critically choose how you learn the material you will be exposed to. You can willfully consider how each concept and theory fits into the bigger picture of your life: how the wardrobe of your mind is equipping you for any and all experiences/adventures you might be put into.

When considering the discipline of management, we have taken the four main functions of the discipline—planning, organizing, leading and controlling—and designed a "do it yourself" wardrobe kit. This kit has been specifically designed for freshman and sophomore students to better grasp the material, retain it for future use, and specifically see a couple examples of ways the learning directly aligns with the biblical narrative and Christian thought. Through our own educational experiences, professional endeavors, academic research and spiritual walks, we have with maturity and time seen the interrelationships of these aspects of life more clearly. We would like to help set you up for success from the beginning. As you begin your life-long learning adventure, you do so in the contemplation of what you are going to do with your life, not as an occupation but as vocation. We hope to equip you for all the opportunities you seek to engage. In a way, we are helping you build the wardrobe of your mind so that you are best equipped, polished, and prepared for whatever you encounter.

The content of each chapter was intentionally designed to consider each reader in light of his or her unique spiritual, professional and individual characteristics. WE haven't provided the answers for you. We have merely provided the blueprints of best learning practices so that you can structure the concepts and theories in a way that is fitting for you and your vocational interests. The questions asked in the reflections have been designed to help develop your critical thinking skills and increase your retention. It is our hope that your learning in this class last far beyond the end of the semester.

Understanding Theories

When you consider all the theories in the world and specifically those in management and leadership—there are a lot of them! Moreover, within these many theories there are "groupings" of those that wrestle with the same problem/issue in the world or society. The fascinating part about that is that we can have five or ten theorists trying to solve the same question, but each are coming from a different perspective, seeing the question through a different lens. Each theorist, seeking to answer those big questions, brings with them their "baggage" including their upbringing, their spirituality, academic training and last but not least, the time period in which they lived. You see, it all is contextualized based on these conditions.

For example, we can ponder today in the 21st millennium how the internet will work without a device. But, in the early 19th century-or even the mid-20th century, contemplating that would have been unheard of as the foundational knowledge required for those questions had not paved the way for thinking about them.

The theorists who write textbooks and research articles are those who have contemplated the rationale for why things are the way they are, and alternatively, how they should be. Each theorist shares common characteristics with the others, which is a propensity to answer an unanswered question with thought that is grounded and substantiated in the research others have done. Those who advance any field of study by asking big questions do not justify their research question and answers leaning solely on their own understanding. They have a willingness to look beyond their immediate scope or discipline in an effort to understand the universality, comprehensiveness and interdependence of the world. While a theory may be situated in a particular field, such as organizational management, ultimately theorists look for ways to explain the world as a whole, not simply one piece of it.

People who generate theories create a compelling argument for how their answer to the unanswered question is at least one way of making meaning out of the question. It's not enough to assert a theory; any theory must be supported by evidence and argument. Theorists who advance their discipline provide support and rationale for the theory they propose and demonstrate how that theory explains some concept. Management theorists focus specifically on how work is structured, how employees' time and abilities are utilized, how employees are motivated (and demotivated) to work, and how employees interact with others, whether it is peers, subordinates, supervisors, or those external to the organization (customers, suppliers, key stakeholders). In addition, management theorists study the way managers make decisions and focus on the need for ethical behavior and assumption of social responsibility on the part of managers.

Abraham Maslow

Let us look at one specific theorist. Take a moment to go to *Exploring Management* and read about Maslow's theory. There you will read about the assumptions that drive his theory and the implications of it for organizational management. But who was Abraham Maslow? Why did he create this theory? How does the person affect the explanation of human behavior? From biographers, we know a great deal about Abraham Maslow's life.

Several factors that shaped how Maslow saw the world around him included when and where he lived, his cultural heritage, his large set of siblings, being brought to American by immigrant parents, and his cultural and faith background. In this case, rather than exploring a bible passage, we are exploring a management theory, but we are using the same process.

Abraham Maslow was born in 1908 of first generation Jewish immigrants who fled Czarist persecution at the turn of the 20th century. He was the oldest of seven children. In his working class neighborhood, he experienced anti-Semitism from teachers and peers alike. Maslow's parents valued education, although they had not completed anything beyond secondary school themselves. While not impoverished, Maslow's family had little beyond necessities. So in looking at his famous Hierarchy of Needs, and the categories within it, one can see how an individual who has not always been blessed with resources, position or privilege would interpret the world. Further, the way one would make assumptions about how humans are motivated would also be a result of this cultural, ideological and philosophical perspective. In addition, it is important to understand that Maslow proposed his theory at a time when the viewpoint of Sigmund Freud and other psychoanalysts was losing its dominant place in psychology. Maslow (1968) claimed that Freud provided the sick half of psychology and it was time to explain the healthy half.

Those who have studied Maslow extensively often criticize his theory as biased toward Western culture and values. The idea of self-actualization may not be applicable to other cultures. Sommers and Satel (2006) claim that Maslow is no longer relevant, although the theory continues to be included in various textbooks on management and psychology.

So, what does Maslow's theory mean to you? Is it relevant? Can you use your understanding of it to be a better manager of others? How does his theory of self-actualization resonant with your understanding of where you want to go and what you want to be?

Moving Forward

This text serves as preparation for the dialogical approach you will encounter in class. It contains chapters on each of the four aspects of management—planning, controlling, organizing, and leading—as well as a chapter on vocation, where we will begin our journey. What we present here is an invitation to discussion and construction, not final words on any particular topic. At the end of each chapter, you have the opportunity to reflect on the material. These reflections will help frame some of your group discussions and are part of your graded work in the course. The chapter's closing sections include:

- Reflection questions designed using the dialogical approach, adult learning theory and other pedagogical best practices

- Graph paper for you to compartmentalize your key takeaways from the chapter as they relate to your life-long learning objectives and vocational interests (building your closet and wardrobe)

- Graph paper for creating relationships between the management concepts discussed in class with others and your own reflections on the material: dialogical approach.

It is our hope that the reflections at the close of each chapter and the discussions you have with classmates are the beginning of dialogue around important ideas, which will provide a chance to you to think about your major in light of your faith.

You may be wondering why we've included graph paper and places to take notes in your text. Why do we want you to write in this book? One reason is that we want you to keep it—not for our sakes but for your own. As a senior, you may find your thoughts as a beginning student to be of interest as you return to them and consider how accurately they reflect your thinking in the present. When you start your first managerial position, you may find it helpful to review the things you learned in this basic class. As is the case in any field, it's hard to break old rules or make new ones unless you understand the foundational ones that govern the field. Pablo Picasso, known best for his cubist art, spent many hours in the discipline of realistic figure drawing before turning to other forms of expression. As a manager, you must understand foundational concepts before individualizing your approach.

It's time to begin writing in your book. On the next page, you'll see a sample start on a "managerial closet" and wardrobe. The person who drew this started with the big questions and put answers to them on "shelves" in the closet. Start your closet by answering those questions for yourself. Yours will look entirely different. That's okay. It's supposed to be about **you**.

After each chapter, you'll be asked to add wardrobe pieces to your closet based on the concepts you encounter in the chapter. Be prepared—it might turn out to be walk-in size!

Sample Closet
(Each box represents a shelf)

ME
- Personal characteristics
- I am loving, caring, a Christian
- Familial support

INDUSTRY
- I have experience in retail
- I hate corruption in work

DISCIPLINE
- Why do companies market cigarettes to kids?
- Why don't schools teach so Enron doesn't happen again?

MY LIFE
- What am I going to do in my life?
- How can I be more Christian?
- What major is right for me?

COMMUNITY
- Why do people have different values?
- How can I help battered women?

SOCIETY
- Where is God in society?
- How do I live in the world but not of the world?

Starting your Management Closet

Start your closet by building shelves that contain your answers to the "big questions" raised in this chapter. Use the two facing pieces of graph paper on the following pages to draw those questions within the context your mental wardrobe, and connect them to academic themes you have been exposed to thus far in your education. In addition, include the start of four different "rooms" which will compartmentalize the four functions of management.

The third piece of graph paper is for you to record insights from your discussion with your peers during class.

On the following pages, start your closet by building shelves that contain your answers to the "big questions" in your life. Include rooms for the functions of management.

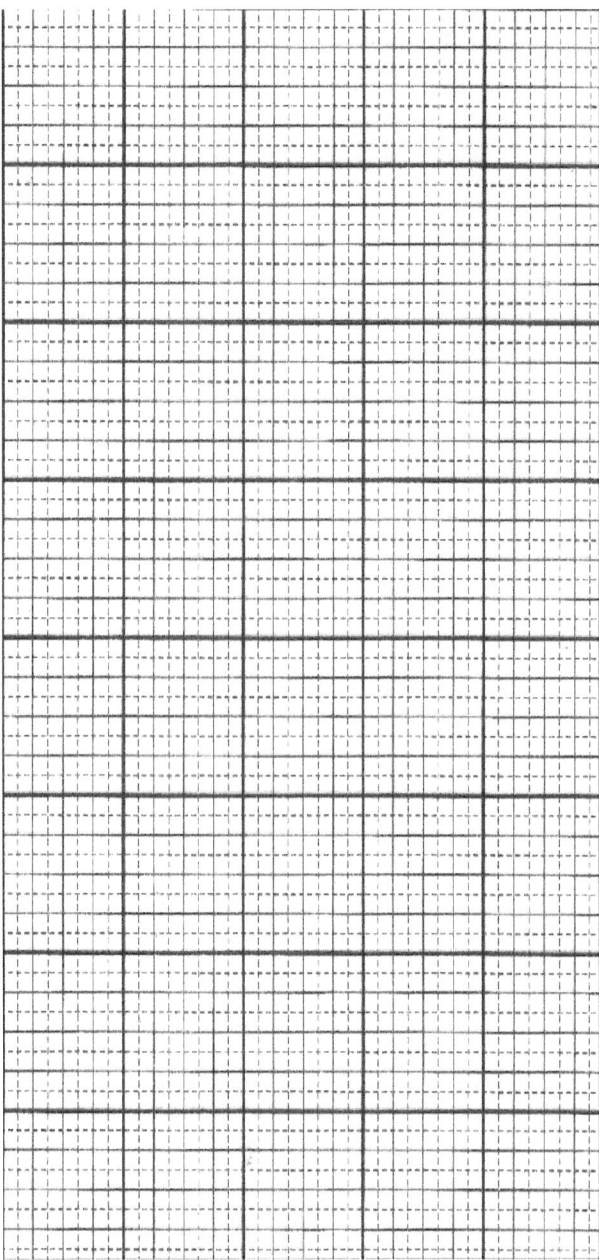

Discussion Takeaways
What did you learn from your peers?

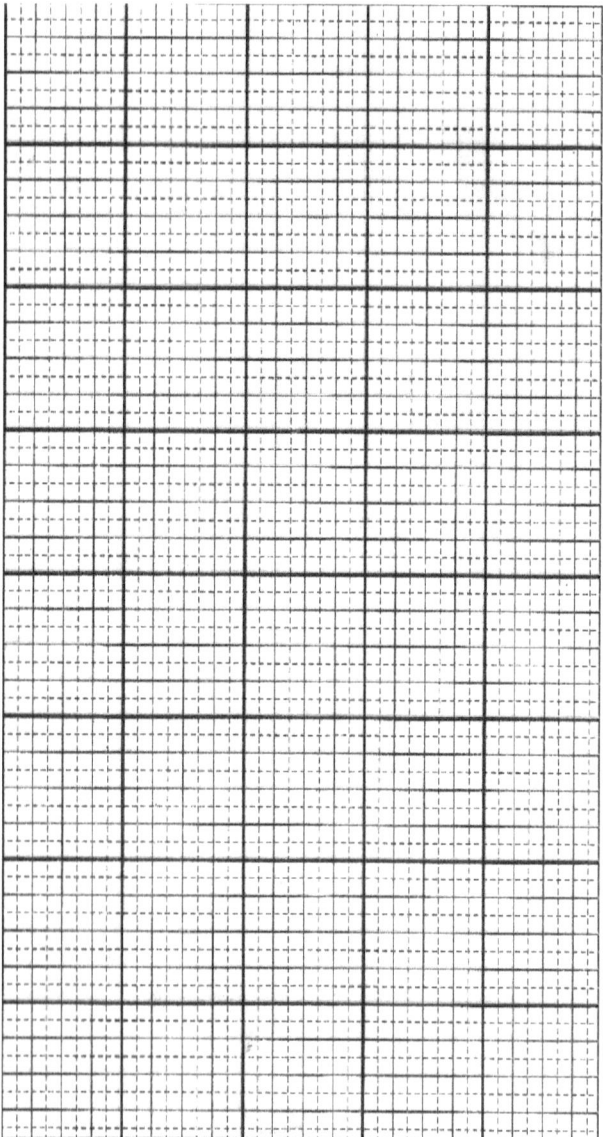

Vocation: God's Calling

Who are You?

If you spend any amount of time on social media, you will see all sorts of inspirational quotes that revolve around being true to yourself. Some are funny, like this one found on a t-shirt: "Always be yourself, unless you can be Batman. Then be Batman." Some are more serious, such as this one from Catherine of Sienna (1347-1380): "Be who you were created to be, and you will set the world on fire." Perhaps the pithiest of these comes from Oscar Wilde (1854-1900): "Be yourself. Everyone else is taken." The question "Who am I?" is common enough. You will ask it of yourself frequently during your university career.

However, the question "Who am I?" is limiting. You might answer it in terms of roles: I am a brother/sister/child/business major, and so forth. You might answer it in terms of your values or attributes: I am kind/passionate/competitive, etc. You might even answer the question in terms of your goals for your career and life. Theories you encounter in this text and in other classes will talk about what it means to live a fulfilled or self-actualized life. The problem is that when we rely on theories of human development and self-actualization, we often get caught up in the idea that somehow, whether or not we are fulfilled or actualized depends upon ourselves. Fowler (2000) calls this

> . . .our most serious modern heresy, the individualistic assumption that we are or can be self-grounded persons. This assumption means believing that we have within us—and are totally responsible for generating from within ourselves—all the resources out of which to create a fulfilled and self-actualized life (italics in original, p. 82).

Whose are You?

What we must do instead is shift our question from "who am I?" to "whose am I?" When we do so, we are answering the question of vocation. As Fowler argues, vocation is not our job or occupation. It is not our profession. It is not our career. "Vocation is the response a person makes with his or her total self to the address of God and to the calling of partnership" (p. 77). In other words, vocation centers on our understanding of who God is, what God wants of us, and how we can use our talents and gifts to build the Kingdom of God on earth. Vocation helps us to answer important questions, such as "Why am I here?" and "What is the meaning of my life?" Through a lens of Christian faith, this active engagement is seen as a spiritual journey through which teachers and students alike aim to discover how God is at work in their lives. When we seek our vocation, fulfillment and self-actualization become the result of our faithfulness as we have responded to God, not the things that we seek at the outset.

Often, when we consider the question of vocation, we start with different bible verses that talk about the call of God on one's life. One oft-quoted verse comes from Isaiah 41:8-10:

> But you, Israel, my servant, Jacob, whom I have chosen, you descendants of Abraham my friend, I took you from the ends of the earth, from its farthest corners I called you. I said, 'You are my servant'; I have chosen you and have not rejected you. So do not fear, for I am with you; do not be dismayed, for I am your God. I will strengthen you and help you; I will uphold you with my righteous right hand.

And, of course, people look to Micah 6:8 for answers:

> He has shown you, O mortal, what is good. And what does the Lord require of

> you? To act justly and to love mercy and
> to walk humbly with your God.

It is important to understand that there is a difference between "calling" and "vocation" as we are using the terms here. When we are called, we hear God's voice providing us direction. God's calling can manifest through our experience of nature, a dream, or a sudden epiphany, but we may also experience it through the wisdom others express. Vocation, on the other hand, is what we do in response to our calling. Calling is an experience; vocation is a behavioral response.

In the midst of asking important questions about what we should do and where we should go, we often get caught up in the terrible fear that somehow, we will miss God's particular purpose for our lives. We fixate on the words of comfort Jeremiah provided to the nation of Israel in 29:11: "For I know the plans I have for you," declares the Lord, "plans to prosper you and not to harm you, plans to give you hope and a future." Friesen (2004) claims that such worry is unjustified. What God asks of us is to live within communities of faith. Friesen argues two important points: First, when we are considering actions the bible explicitly addresses, we need to be sure we are following God's commands (e.g., telling the truth, paying our taxes, loving our neighbor as ourselves, and so on). Second, if there is no specific guidance on a particular subject (e.g., what you should major in), then you are free to make your own decisions as long as they are within the scope of what God calls everyone to do and be. Any decision made within that scope is acceptable to God (p. 179).

Now before you drop this text and decide we are clueless about faith and what faith calls us to, understand that we believe the idea of vocation helps us make those important decisions as we are working to place ourselves within God's call to humanity. It is not that God does not care whether you become an accountant or a minister (although becoming an embezzler would certainly be out of the question). It is that vocation helps you to recognize how you will present your entire self to God and God's calling. Theologian Frederick Beuchner argues that vocation is found where one's greatest passion meets a great need in the world.

The contemplation of vocation within the context of this particular course helps you to understand how, even if you do not become a business leader or manager, the principles of management will inform your response to God's calling. In addition, when you encounter other courses and view them through the lens of faith toward an understanding of vocation, you will begin to see how all of your education (really!)

leads you to a deeper understanding of your path in life and the ways in which you will serve God and others.

The Gifts of Vocation

Perhaps the most important idea to take away from Fowler's work on vocation concerns the gifts that embracing our vocation gives to us. Fowler identifies seven of them. First, when we embrace our vocation, we strive for excellence that is not based on competition with others. Rather, we work toward excellence in what we do regardless of what others are doing.

Second, when we embrace vocation, we stop worrying about whether we will be the first to do something, or whether, somehow or some way, someone else will fulfill the destiny God chose for us. Our lives are justified in vocation and our response to God's calling, not in particular achievements.

Third, and perhaps the most freeing, we are able to rejoice in what others have been gifted with and can see the grace within them. Rather than comparing ourselves to others, we celebrate and rejoice in all that God has blessed in others and ourselves. We need not be jealous of what others have; we need only employ the gifts and graces God has given to us.

Fourth, in embracing our vocation, we are

liberated from the need to be everything to everyone. We do not need to be good at everything. We do not need to know everything. We do need to know how to seek help when we are unequipped, and to seek answers when we have questions. And, because we have been freed from being everything, we experience the fifth gift, which is having balance in the way we invest our time and energy. Someone who works to the point of exhaustion is not serving God.

A sixth of vocation is being "freed from the tyranny of time" (p. 84). So often, we think of our lives as working toward meeting goals on a timetable—by the time you're 22, you should have your Bachelor's degree; by the time you're 30, you should be married and have children; by the time you're in your 50s, you should be prepared for retirement. Instead of having to check off experiences and achievements on a list, we see instead that we are called into time by God. Our lives are not segmented pieces but whole experiences that lead us to joyous reunion with our Creator when our Creator calls us home.

Finally, and most importantly, we leave behind the idea that our vocation is a one-time choice that we must live with until our death. Our vocation is open to change. As we grow and live and respond to God, we understand that vocation may change and that such change is not frightening. As Isaiah says, God has chosen us. When we walk with God throughout our lives, we know we have the strength to face both stability and change in our vocation. Rather than limiting ourselves to the skills we have learned through education and training, we can focus on what God has given us and how we can use all those combined experiences and our education for God's use. Sometimes vocation will be clear to us immediately. At other times, we will find that our vocation comprises experiences intertwined with a myriad of things that we could never, ever, have dreamed up on our own.

Why do we begin with the idea of vocation? As you will see in the following chapters, we have looked to those in the field of organizational management who have made it their vocation, and in so doing, have broadened our understanding of the field. In each of the four areas of management, we present the story of someone who demonstrated that skill through embracing the vocation to which they were called. What is God calling you to do?

Reflection One: Vocation

Instructions: Answer each question using a minimum of 50 words and a maximum of 150 words. Please use the word count function in your word processing program. Type your answers and hand in a hard copy of the assignment on the due date.

What experiences have you had with the idea of vocation? Is the way in which you have thought about vocation similar to or different from the ideas you just encountered by reading this chapter?

As you reflect on your past experiences with vocation, what conclusions can you draw? What have you learned from your experiences?

Identify a bible verse or a quote that helps you understand how you will approach your vocation and live it. Why is this verse or quote so important to you?

In the coming semester, what are your plans to explore the concept of vocation? Name at least two things you intend to do this semester to improve your understanding of your vocation.

Adding Vocation to your Management Closet

What are three things you are most interested in and/or passionate about that need to be a part of your your mental wardrobe blueprint? Use the two facing pieces of graph paper on the following pages to draw those three things within the context your mental wardrobe, and connect them to academic themes you have been exposed to thus far in your education. Make any connections you can at this time to the four functions of management.

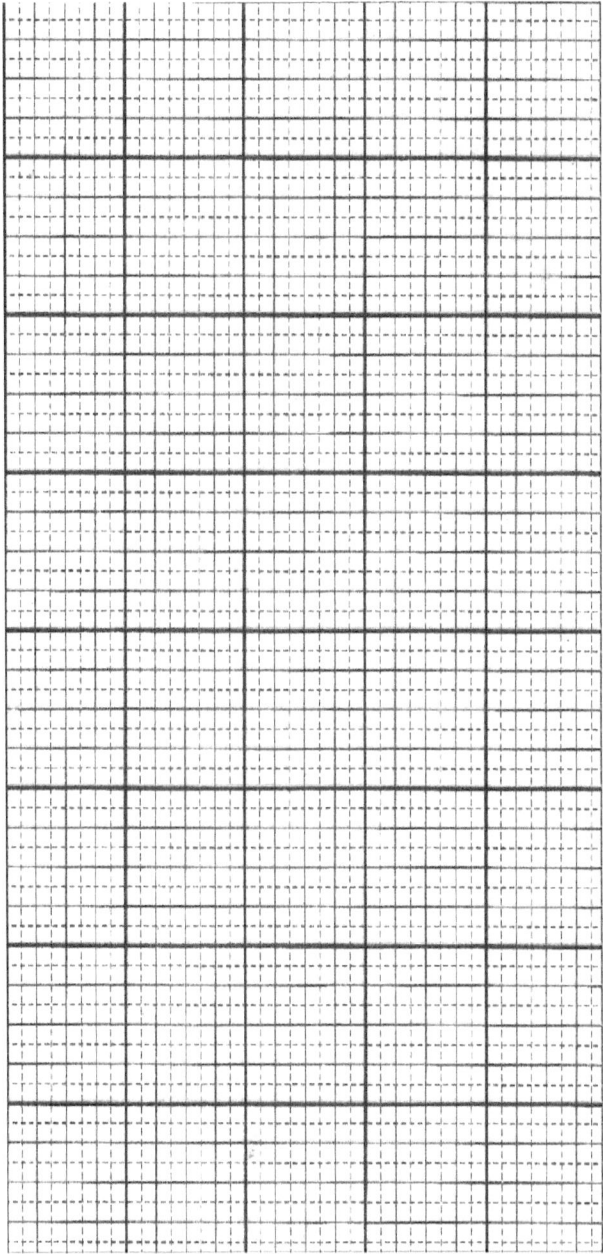

Discussion Takeaways
What did you learn from your peers?

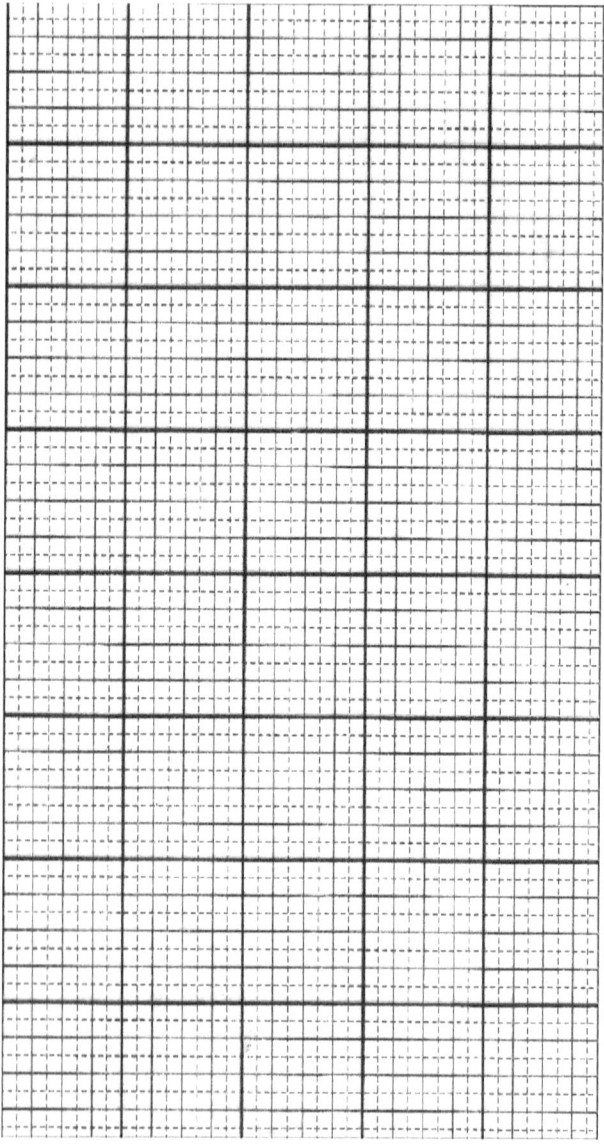

Planning

Every management textbook explains the principles and values of planning. In its most narrow sense, planning is the forethought or consideration put into future action; it is the thinking before the doing. Every model of planning that you'll read about is derived from this basic definition.

As you have read in your textbook, there are three basic types of planning. Strategic planning revolves around long-term goals and creates vision for the organization. Operational or tactical planning develops steps to implement a strategic plan. Functional planning revolves around determining how different parts of the organization will take part in fulfilling the strategic plan.

God's Planning

When we look at planning from a Christian perspective, we see the importance of it from the very beginning of God's work. From the way in which creation progresses in the thoughtful consideration of each day, we see specific events which shaped the universe and humanity. Through the unfolding of God's word and eventual plan of salvation, we are provided an explanation of the purpose of creation and salvation. As Christ-followers, created in God's image, we have planning and strategic execution and measurement inherent in our DNA. We were created within a master plan, intended to be co-laborers in that plan. Every human creation was designed to participate in the co-laboring with Christ: we were intended to be in relationship with him, and our human nature in many respects reflects that intended purpose of our being.

The creation of light, the seas, the earth, and the earth's inhabitants is itself ordered. Why, for instance, were the birds and fowl created before the beasts on the earth? Any ideas? Wenham (1998) notes that this question is complex, and that to understand the order of creation, it requires we delve into the cultural context of the era: what the people were like, what their society and communities were like, and what their thinking was like at that time. From an ordering perspective, we believe that the fish and fowl were created first in order to provide sustenance for the game and eventually humans that were later created. It was the master plan of the eco system.

Let's look further at the order of creation. John 1:1 states "In the beginning was the word, and the word was with God and the word was God

(NIV)." From that point, the days evolve in a developmental process that leads us to a day of rest: Sabbath. Sabbath is the end of the original creation cycle. This concept will mean something different to each person based on their theology of a new or old earth, divinely inspired texts, or a carrying of ancient stories told from generation to generation. Regardless of which of these lenses you look at the scripture through, one thing is constant, the declaration of the Sabbath is a significant end to the cycle.

In addition, the ordering of creation was, in part, directed by what the ending creation needed: humans' needs. For example, what would it have been like for humans and mammals to roam the earth without a protein source? Think about that for a second. Now, let us think about what it would be like to bake bread if you turned the oven on, and you had not activated the yeast? Or, you were manufacturing soft drinks without the CO_2? From a managerial perspective, we need to know what the end goal is in order to create the mechanisms for optimal performance and productivity. As managers and leaders, we typically focus on our customers' needs and work backwards in product development and the ensuing manufacturing of those products.

But, let's go back to the first verse of the first chapter of the first book in the first testament.

In the beginning was... From a managerial perspective, that means to us that something WAS. There was a current state before the activity of creation. God existed, and the Word existed. When we explore biblical experts understanding of the bible through texts such as commentaries, we find that "was" is far broader reaching than just God and the Word. In fact, Old Testament theologians have written volumes on what "was" before the chronicle of Genesis was penned. "IS" and "AM" are explanations of what it means to have God and the Word in existence, outside of creation. For managers it means that this is a benchmark: a place where we use a measure to gauge performance with because we seek to use a starting place by which to gauge productivity and profitability in an environment that is always changing—and unpredictable.

It also means that we accept that things exist before we start measuring. As was the case with us, the authors, your parents probably measured you as you were growing up and marked it on a wall. Your parents may have done it regularly, such as at the beginning of the school year, or sporadically, when they noticed you had grown. And even though the cycle of measurement marked on a wall most likely did not begin until you were able to stand, you existed, and had height before you started being quantified on the wall. When you were born, your height was measured in length because you couldn't stand. As managers we often assume that some activity, growth or production occurred before we begin quantifying the measurement of it.

Policies and Procedures

Policies and procedures are an important part of the planning process. What purpose do they serve? Why do we have them? Are they critical for organizations? The purpose for HR policies and procedures is to provide guidelines for behavior and consequences for not behaving consistently with the organization's rules.

Consider Micah 6:8: "He has shown you, O mortal, what is good. And what does the Lord require of you: To act justly and to love mercy and to walk humbly with your God (NIV)." This verse provides context for how to live out the concept of policies and procedures but doesn't actually specify the consequences for failing to do so.

Let us look at an Old Testament perspective on policies and procedures. In Exodus, we receive the Ten Commandments. We commonly understand these to be laws that are enduring, regardless of time or situation, which are mandates of God to humanity. But, are these commandments simply a list of obligations and prohibitions?

The Ten Commandments are much more than a list of rules. Von Rad (2001) sees them as "ordinances for common, ordinary human life 'commandments', sometimes as legal ordinances (parts of the Book of the Covenant and of Deuteronomy), and sometimes as ordinances for the intricate sphere of worship" (pg. 188). He further describes the Ten Commandments as "the conception of the traditions (Israel's traditions) as documents narrating a history with God" (p. 188). A close reading of the Old Testament reveals many instances when the Israelites strayed from the commandments, and the consequences of doing so are often severe.

Similar to the Ten Commandments, modern society creates ordinances for the well-being of society and its members. When we consider an organization as the unit of analysis, we have insight into the ordinances for those in the internal and external environment. Specifically, organizations create a history with all their stakeholders by using policies and procedures. From a Christian perspective, there are three key determining factors in the development of policies and procedures: humility, justice and mercy. Can you think of a planning process you have experienced that enveloped humility? Justice? Mercy? Can you compare that with another experience of yours where those qualities were not exercised? In considering the two experiences, is it possible for you to identify how that might have changed your followership? How did it change your perception of the leader and/or the organization? Is there a management theory (either classical or behavioral) that likens itself to your perceptions of those positive and negative experiences with humility, justice and mercy in the planning process?

Like other prophets of the Old Testament, Micah was not always the most valued member in his community. But, he carried the prophetic word of the LORD to the Israelites. When reading Micah 6:8, we see that he's writing the content of what God has done to provide what is good for humanity—in the context of what had already occurred and been scribed to and for the Israelites: the exodus, the 10 commandments, the settlement of Canaan, and so on. And, now in this tiny book, we see Micah speaking God's word to the Israelites in His command to them: act justly, love mercy and walk humbly. Note that it's written as a requirement for all of us as humans (reference "mortal"). Note also that Micah refers to how we are to know these things, because God has shown us. So, within the Old Testament, what examples can you recall that are evidence of how God has shown us about justice, mercy and humility? What historical events had occurred by that time that the Israelites would have as a part of their cultural narrative that would inform their values, practices, and desires?

We were created as a part of an ordered plan, and we have been instructed to work and live in an ordered plan. Are there examples of every type of plan and of every type of concept of planning in the biblical narrative? Likely. Why? Because it's a part of the human condition. It is a part of how we were designed to engage with creation within the confines of time as we serve and co-labor for a living God who is outside of time.

Reflection Two: Planning

Instructions: Answer each question using a minimum of 50 words and a maximum of 150 words. Please use the word count function in your word processing program. Type your answers, print and staple it, and hand in a hard copy of the assignment on the due date.

1. What experiences have you had with the concept or practice of planning? How has God brought the skill of planning into your life? What opportunities have you had to plan? Is the way in which you have thought about planning similar to or different from the ideas you just encountered? Identify how your thoughts are similar or different.

2. As you reflect on your past experiences with planning, what conclusions can you

draw? For example, at what point were you brought into a planning process. What have you learned from your experiences? What does good planning look like? What does ineffective planning look like? What policies and procedures did/might you recommend based on the experience you had?

3. Identify a bible verse or a quote (please be sure to identify where a verse or quote comes from) that helps you understand how you will approach the skill of planning and live it. Why is this verse or quote so important to you?

4. In the coming semester, what are your plans to explore the concept of planning? Name at least two things you intend to do this semester to better understand the skill of planning.

Adding Planning to your Management Closet

Draw a room for planning and identify the helpful and harmful entities to your planning process. Identify those practices, things, people who have best practices in planning, etc. and put them in the room. Outside of the planning room, in the margins of your blueprint (i.e. page), denote the items that create a cumbersome environment for you in your planning.

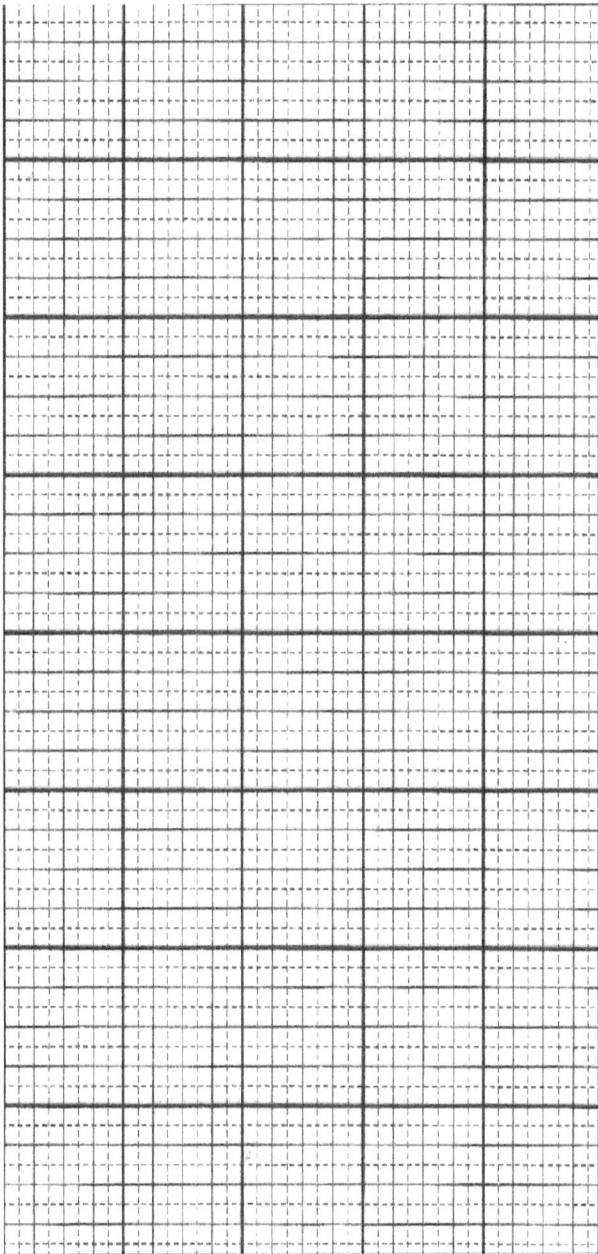

Discussion Takeaways
What did you learn from your peers?

Controlling

Control in the Secular Sense

From a management perspective, "control" is a clearly understood concept. Managerial control focuses on ensuring that actions taken by members of the organization serve the overall mission and goals of the organization. Control is achieved by the creation of expected outcomes for employees through their knowledge of organizational goals and the rewards for achieving those goals (as well as the sanctions that can be applied if they don't). While the achievement of managerial control can be complicated, understanding of it in organizational management is not.

In everyday use, though, the word "control" elicits a variety of meanings. When you think of the word "control," what comes to mind? Control is one of those peculiar concepts that plagues us as humans. Control is a good thing when we have it but a bad thing when we don't, especially when we're dealing with someone else who does have it. A person who is "controlling" generally isn't seen as someone who is pleasant to be around. Someone who is a "control freak" is seen the same way. We don't like to feel out of control when it comes to events in our lives. In fact, control is such an important idea in our society that a simple Google search of the term generates 2.9 BILLION results. Our need for control and its importance to us is reflected in such phrases as

Who has the conn?

Who's on first?

Who's got the ball?

Who stole my cheese?

Who's the boss?

Who's in the driver's seat?

God's Control

From a Christian perspective, none of these make sense, and none of these are control from a theologically-grounded approach. As people who choose to worship God and put faith in God's plan, control is something we need to re-think. One way of thinking about control is to consider how we pray. Do we ask or demand things of God? Do we really seek guidance or confirmation of what we already think? As you read these words from the Lord's Prayer (Matthew 6:9-13), a passage of the bible you probably memorized as a youth and can still recite easily, think carefully about the implications of these words from a managerial viewpoint.

Our Father, who art in heaven, hallowed be they name. Thy kingdom come, thy will be done on earth as it is in heaven.

From the very start of the prayer, we are reminded of the One who has control. It is not us. It is God. In addition, control isn't simply about the way we use the resources we have been given, but it calls us to be reverent of and have respect for the talents, servants, and processes that have been entrusted to us. Further, managerial control, when viewed through God's economy, is about finding ways to bring a kingdom perspective to feedforward, concurrent, and feedback mechanisms.

Give us today our daily bread

This part of the prayer is not only giving thanks for what we have been given to eat, but also accepting and being thankful for the resources under our discretion. As managers we are provided human capital, assets, finances, and processes. Rather than focus on the limitations of what we have been given, we need to figure out how we can best use what we do have and work to increase those resources without shortchanging others in the organization or the customers we serve.

And forgive us our debts, as we also have forgiven our debtors

We have been forgiven so much, particularly when we recognize that all sin separates us from God. While as humans we tend to think of "bigger" and "smaller" sins, from a theological standpoint all sin is the same in that it separates us from God. Only one sin, blasphemy against the Holy Spirit, is unforgivable. This is not an argument that all sins should have the same consequences in relationships and organizations, but it is an assertion that, as all of us sin daily, none of us has justification for condemning another for what he or she has done. We are, however, expected to be part of a system that is caring, just and merciful. (Micah 6:8)

In management, the grace we have been given should be reflected in the grace we extend to others. We should provide direction, communication, and follow-up for our direct reports, peers, and supervisors. We should be understanding of human error and look for ways to correct it without embarrassment or blame. When things don't go as we expect, we should have contingency plans that allow, to whatever extent is possible, a smooth transition to an alternate pathway.

And lead us not into temptation but deliver us from

the evil one.

There are so many ways in which we can stray from managing "God's way". In efforts to save time or money, we may think it appropriate to diminish service levels or skip processes that feel cumbersome, time consuming, and/or costly. Such actions are ultimately self-defeating for both the organization and ourselves. In addition, we are called to remain ethical and honest in all our doings; we must remain above reproach. Finally, we need to do our best to act in ways that don't lead those we supervise to engage in unethical practices themselves.

For thine is the kingdom, the power, and the glory forever.

The power we have and the control we exercise, is God's, not ours. We control only what is already in God's hands, and only what God has given us dominion over. And when we succeed, we remember that it is only through the grace of God and what God has given us that we are able to do so.

Control and Decision Making

Given this understanding of control from a theological perspective, how then, do we put it into practice? What kind of process can we use to help us make decisions that reflect God's economy and not our own need for control and power? In your textbook, you will see a decision making model that managers can use. It has five steps:

1. Identify the problem. What are we called to do? What is presenting itself? For example, you may be experiencing delays in the delivery of product because manufacturing does not have accurate information about the number of units needed.

2. Generate and evaluate alternative solutions. What are the possible ways that the problem can be addressed? Do you need better communication? Do you need a digital tracking system that the sales force and manufacturing can access so that information is shared in a timelier manner? Do you need a temporary workforce that can come in for high production periods?

3. Decide on preferred course of action. You decide that the problem is communication flow and work on ways to improve that.

4. Implement the decision. You implement a plan for better communication between sales and manufacturing.

5. Evaluate results. You determine whether the particular solution you selected addresses the problem or whether you need to find alternative ways to address it.

As managers, we can follow the process directed to us by Him in the Lord's Prayer through its modification, applying the concepts to managerial roles and tasks:

- We pray for direction

- We received direction and attribute it as an answer to prayer

- We act upon the inspired word, giving God the glory

- We assist others in accomplishing their role in that action

- We praise God for opportunity to co-labor with him.

- We rest. Yes, we rest. We reflect, we measure, we assess. But, we rest.

It's important to think of this process as cyclical, because as our proficiency in prayer and understanding God's will improves, our ability to engage in the process also improves. Visually, the process looks like this:

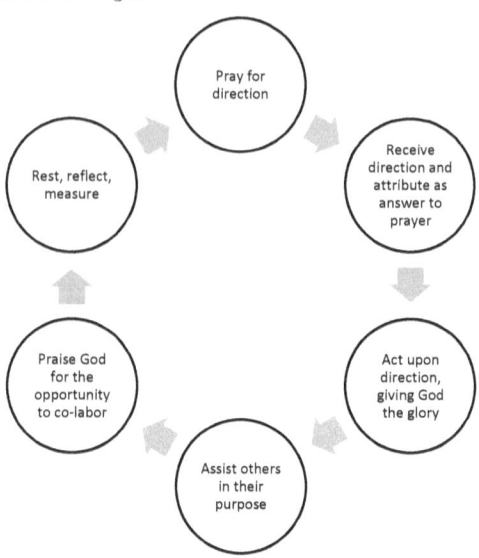

Types of Control

As you read in your textbook, managerial control can be internal, external, and bureaucratic; control may also be enforced through clan control. Internal control is exercised by employees through self-discipline as they approach their tasks. External control is exercised through the way in which employees are supervised as well as through the design of administrative systems. Bureaucratic control is exercised through policies, procedures, job descriptions, and so on. Finally, clan control occurs through peer pressure and social norms.

Managers must strive to help employees develop internal control. We believe that this can be accomplished by living out the words Paul wrote in Galatians 5:13: "You, my brothers and sisters, were called to be free. But do not use your freedom to indulge the flesh; rather, serve one another humbly in love." If we work to empower and develop our employees, and to find ways for them to expand their knowledge and understanding, internal control increases. Our employees become committed to the task and to the organization and, for the most part, will begin to act in ways that are mutually beneficial to themselves and to the organization.

In supervision, we recognize that we are co-laborers with those we manage. Status as a manager does not give us permission to engage in selfish actions or retain special privileges. Freedom is associated with power, but we must use that power appropriately, with the right motive and attitude, and recognize the actual source of our control. In other words, freedom is intended to provide opportunity to humbly serve one another. Freedom, or control over situations (resources, employees, and processes) is not about the "me" rather it is about the "we". Serving others is the purpose and end result of control in organizations. Our purpose is to further God's kingdom, and that is best done by developing systems so that "God's will" can be done in all things, in all places, for all people, for God's purpose.

So, when we acknowledge that God has the conn, and that we have a function within that realm of understanding-it totally changes what control means. Control is the way in which we help others evolve and grow into their vocations. Control is the way in which we act within organizations to ensure that ethical practices persist. Control is the way in which we bring God's kingdom into fruition.

Reflection Three: Control

Read the story of Exodus, particularly chapters 3 – 7:6. Note how God interacts with Moses and how Moses subsequently interacts with Pharaoh. Limit your responses to 150 words or less for each question.

1. How does God use: a) internal, b) external, and c) bureaucratic controls to guide Moses' behavior? How does Moses use each of them in turn when he interacts with Pharaoh? Use both a commentary and your text to explicate your understanding of each control example.

2. As you reflect on intentionality in which God and Moses used managerial controls, think about the ways in which those you have worked for, or family members such as parents or guardians,

have used similar controls to guide your behavior. Provide an example of each control mechanism (internal, external and bureaucratic) and how those controls were used to guide you.

3. Evaluate the effectiveness of various types of managerial controls. Which do you think are most effective and why? Which do you think are the least effective and why? Substantiate your reflection using concepts from the text and personal examples.

4. What are some ways you can increase your effectiveness in the use of managerial controls that reflect consistency with your terminal values.

Adding Control to your Management Closet

On the graph paper immediately following this chapter, contemplate the control function. Include the key concepts of control that you resonate with, and those which you would like to further explore and/or develop a greater understanding of.

List the resources you need to develop control competencies. Make a note of those items that reduce your ability to control, placing them in the margins or outside of the room.

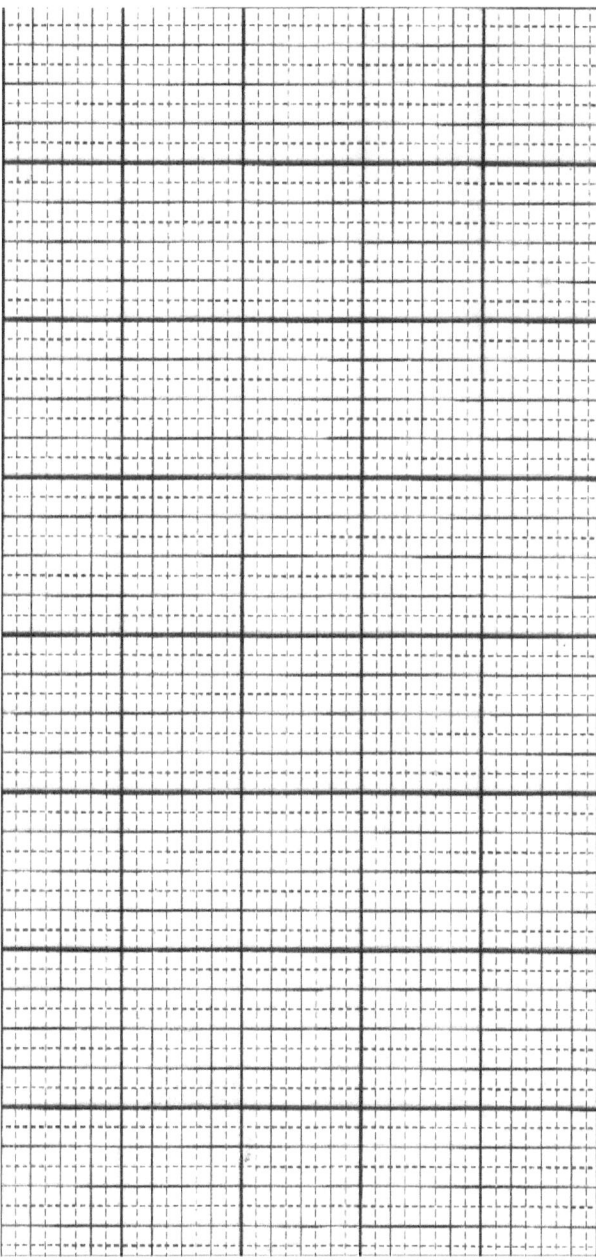

Discussion Takeaways
What did you learn from your peers?

Organizing

The Importance of Organizing

If you have trouble organizing yourself, you are not alone. A plethora of resources are available for those who need help–everything from books, seminars, systems are available to assist the organizationally-challenged. On the other hand, there are some people who are so organized that it's almost scary. They have places for everything, and anything they use is promptly put away when the task is finished. Things are labeled, folded, and sorted. They live by the mantra "A place for everything and everything in its place."

Whether you are someone needing help or someone who already has a system, thinking about organizing in this way is only a very small part of what it means to fulfill the organizing function as a manager. As you read in your text, the management function of organizing includes creating organizational structures and the division of labor, and encompasses such concepts as formal and informal structures, silos, span of control, and empowerment.

A practice ties all the concepts of organizing

together— mindfulness. Not only do we have to organize ourselves in ways that work for us, we need to organize tasks in ways that work for others as well. Managers and leaders need to design and oversee systems that balance the need for profitability, efficiency, and effectiveness, while at the same time adapting such systems so that those they supervise can perform to the best of their ability. This tension in balancing such priorities is often found in the trade-offs managers make between tasks and relationships.

When we look at task-oriented people, those who are wired naturally to task assessment and completion, the mindset is one of the "job". Such individuals focus on the task and its achievement regardless of the specific people in the situation. When emerging managers who are task-minded enter the scene, they often try to set the system and the people in a way that allows them to complete their own tasks as efficiently as possible.

Alternatively, when we look at relationship-oriented people, we find that they are more naturally bent towards the people in the process and the people in the structure. They also are keenly aware of their own and others' linkages and relationships within the organizational structure itself. Relationship-oriented people are the folks who work better in tasks after relationships have been established. As relationship-oriented managers seek to understand and set up systems based on relationships and task achievement-but the relationship and dynamics of those relationships are key to the structure setting for them.

Regardless of whether a manager is task-oriented or relationship-oriented, it is important to ensure that these low-level task and relational needs of their followers and peers are valued and addressed. By addressing direct reports' task/relationship needs early on in the working relation and or project it increases employee motivation and satisfaction which directly translates to output and productivity.

Organizing as a Christian Practice

So, for the case of examining organization as a way to interpret and find meaning in our work as Christians, let us consider some of the characteristics that the organizing concepts have in common: care for people, responsibility, efficiency and effectiveness. How can individuals act Christianly in their work with respect to the organization's structure and systems under their dominion? How can they foster the same Christian responses from those who are working within that system? It is not enough for the motives of the manager to be correct. If the system itself was created to be self-serving, it would make it difficult for a manager to exercise his or her faith in that situation. If the system was designed to allow profits to be manipulated in an unethical way which were invisible to employees within the system, a manager would face even greater difficulties. What if the system was created in such a way that the bureaucracy was so tight that there was no avenue for employees to bring awareness of unethical behavior to the attention of management? Conversely, what if the system was designed so loosely that nobody actually knew what they were responsible and held accountable for in their evaluations? Both these situations are plausible futures for you. How will you work within the system to improve the justice within it and the ability of your subordinates to complete their work in a way that enriches them while benefiting the organization?

These are just a few examples of the "human side" of organization. But at the core of organizing we see a need to create and maintain a system that allows people and processes to function. It's about framing the organization so that people can be most effective and efficient within that created system. And, the side benefit to the human side of organizations is the strengthening of workplace spirituality.

Organizing God's People

There are many examples of God and God's people setting the foundations for how a community should operate, how a church should be organized, and how families should dwell in harmony. Each are examples of organizing people so that they flourish in their particular environment. A more general passage that will aid us in unpacking the concept of understanding the people within the environment/structure that we're seeking to create is James 3:17: "But the wisdom from above is first of all pure. It is also peace loving, gentle at all times, and willing to yield to others. It is full of mercy and good deeds. It shows no favoritism and is always sincere."

When James wrote this book he was writing specifically about living a life of Christian faith, and how that life of faith is a daily practice. This practice of Christian faith is evident in thoughts, actions and deeds, and the fruit of the Christian faith is consistent with the promises outlined in the biblical narrative. The actions of our lives (as it pertains to ourselves, the way we engage with others, and the way we value and use resources) are evidence of faith.

One of the things lacking in this passage of biblical wisdom is a mention of justice. But, as we look at the attributes James does mention—being peace loving, gentle, yielding, and full of mercy and good deeds, lacking favoritism and always sincere—we can see that each of these has justice as a component within it. So, let us consider how a manager with a value system including equity would view Godly wisdom and implore Christ-followers to seek after it. Through the eyes of justice, we see that such a management style is pure, peace loving, always gentle, and willing to yield. What management theory do you think of? Which ones seem to resonate with these godly attributes (pure, peace loving, gentle and yielding)?

Mary Follett

One theorist whose work reflects a work ethic centered on values is Mary Follett. Follett considered humanity to be a work in process, and focused on training and equipping others based on their capacity, while providing an environment in which they could flourish. Follett was raised in a Quaker home and community. The values she was taught as a child and the practices she developed around her spirituality encompassed the values of simplicity, peace, integrity, community, equality and stewardship. In her teenage years, due to her father's death, it was incumbent upon her to take on more financial responsibility for the household- delaying her education. She persevered, and graduated with studies in economics, government, law and philosophy. After school, she began working in a position we currently would refer to as a social worker. She then expanded her influence and worked at the community level, helping to organize local systems to meet the needs of the people. When we focus on the aspects of wisdom James identifies, being peace loving, gentle, and yielding to others, we can see how Follett's spiritual and educational experiences framed her understanding and how her life of faith was demonstrated in specific, behavioral and attitudinal ways.

It is no wonder that as a management theorist, Follett is known for understanding individuals in light of their nuclear, community and societal networks. Further, we can see the direct link between care for community with the concept of social responsibility. She was one of the first to actually conceptualize social responsibility, which is the consideration and responsibility one takes on behalf of their social environment to enable others to thrive in meaningful ways.

Though most of us will not be known for winning a Nobel Prize, setting a world record, or finding the cure for a dreadful disease, we each— just like Follett—can practice the living out of our faith in such a way that it positively impacts those around us in a Christ-like way. In order to walk through how Follett accomplished this, let us take the time to practice self-reflection as living our faith is actuated today.

Reflection Four: Organizing

Instructions: Answer each question using a minimum of 50 words and a maximum of 100 words. Please use the word count function in your word processing program, to ensure that your responses are within the required parameters, and include the word count after each answer. Type your answers and hand in a stapled hard copy of the assignment on the due date.

1. Name three (3) management theories that come to mind as you contemplate these qualities: purity, peace-loving, gentle, willingness to yield? Provide two sentences for each theory, indicating why you have identified them in this manner.

2. Using your own experience as a manager (or as a subordinate to a particular manager) indicate the behaviors listed below. Be sure to describe the situation and the behavior in specific terms. What exactly did you or the manager do that exemplified these attributes?

    a. Two examples of how your direct reports (or your managers) could see evidence of faith in behavior.

b. One example of your (or your manager's) willingness to yield to others.

c. One example of your (or your manager's) gentleness.

d. One example of your (or your manager's) sincerity.

Adding Organizing to your Management Closet

Construct the organization room and identify 5-10 key "ah-ha" concepts of organizing and how you envision using them vocationally.

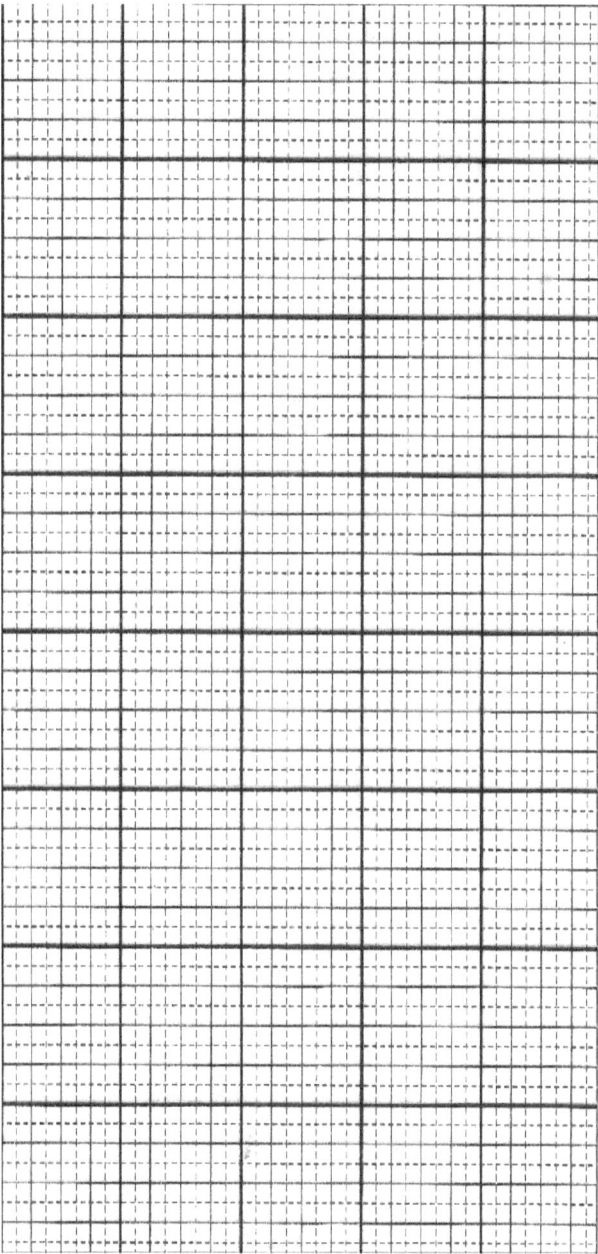

Discussion Takeaways
What did you learn from your peers?

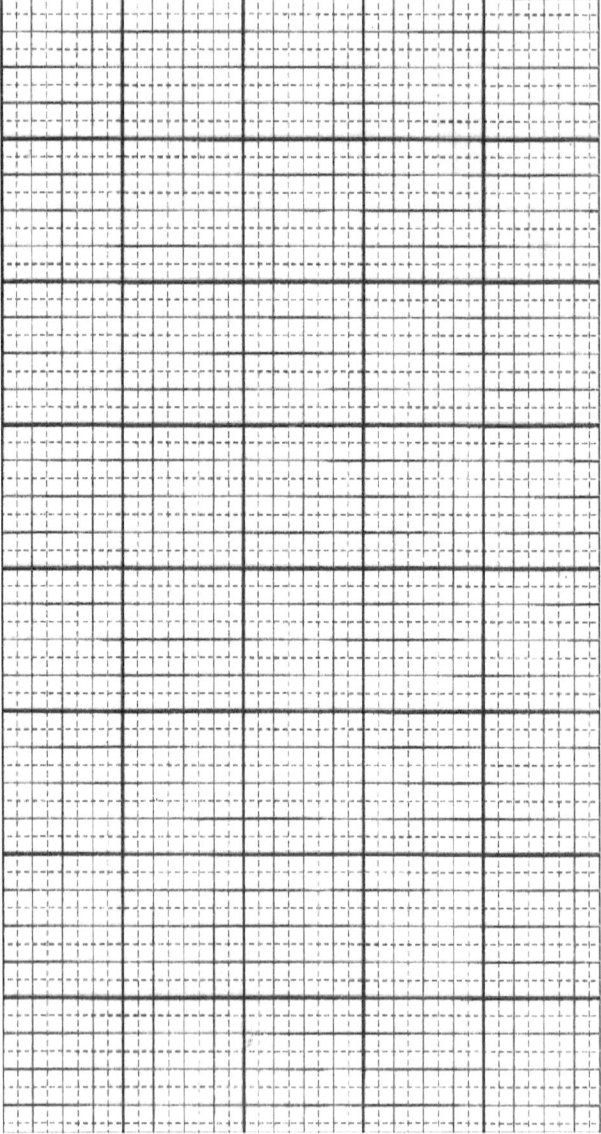

Leading

Leadership: Always a Topic of Interest

If you want to read about leadership, you have a wealth of options available. One online book site boasts approximately 173,000 books on the topic, with about 3,900 on the topic of Christian leadership. Your textbook discusses leadership as a function of management, and argues that leaders use positional and personal power to achieve influence, bring vision to the organization, have different traits, and use different styles. Perhaps the most significant discussions in your chapter revolve around emotional intelligence, servant leadership, and moral leadership. How are these faith issues?

Emotional Intelligence and Faith

Emotionally intelligent people understand themselves and others. They are self-aware and can judge the impact they have on others. They are aware of the demands of social situations, they control their impulses, and they manage their relationships successfully. The writer of Proverbs gives a great deal of advice on self-management and the effect we have on others. In the New Testament, we have the epistles of

Paul that instruct us in a similar manner. Most of Paul's epistles have to do with relationships between people and leaders and how everyone should act together for the sake of the gospel. Consider these words of advice from both testaments.

Self-awareness	Romans 12:3: For by the grace given me I say to every one of you: Do not think of yourself more highly than you ought, but rather think of yourself with sober judgment, in accordance with the faith God has distributed to each of you.
Social awareness	Romans 10:31-33: So whether you eat or drink or whatever you do, do it all for the glory of God. Do not cause anyone to stumble, whether Jews, Greeks or the church of God— even as I try to please everyone in every way. For I am not seeking my own good but the good of many, so that they may be saved.
Self-	Proverbs 4:22-27: Above all else, guard your heart, for

management	everything you do flows from it. Keep your mouth free of perversity; keep corrupt talk far from your lips. Let your eyes look straight ahead; fix your gaze directly before you. Give careful thought to the paths for your feet and be steadfast in all your ways. Do not turn to the right or the left; keep your foot from evil.
Relationship management	Romans 10:23-24: "I have the right to do anything," you say—but not everything is beneficial. "I have the right to do anything"—but not everything is constructive. No one should seek their own good, but the good of others.

We believe that emotionally intelligent people are so because they take the gospel to heart. They know who they are and have a realistic view of their capabilities and talents; more importantly, they know whose they are. They are aware of the demands of social situations, and while not following those conventions blindly, they know how to be faithful without being obnoxious about it. They control their impulses and understand that there is a time to speak and a time to be silent. And they cultivate relationships with others, not simply with others comfortable to them but those who expand their worlds. The bottom line—it is hard to be successful in the leadership function of management without building and using emotional intelligence.

Servant Leadership

Servant leadership is a term heard frequently in Christian institutions and often used by people who have not actually explored the concept fully. Part of the problem is that many who say they are committed to servant leadership continue to hold tightly to the power that comes with position, and continue to wield that authoritative power alongside rewarding and coercive power behaviors. A servant leader is one because he or she is committed to the goal of the organization, and because he or she is committed to leading and influencing through personal power. A servant leader uses personal power to advance the goals of the organization, as well as helping those below him or her to achieve their goals within the context of the organization.

A servant leader is not a slave to others. A servant leader is one who is committed to the well-being of the organization and its members. This commitment is tempered, of course, by wisdom. Some people are not ready or have a wish to be empowered. The servant leader adapts to the needs of the followers while keeping a constant focus on organizational goals.

In many ways, a servant leader best exists in an organization that emphasizes good "followership" as well. Once a rarely discussed concept, the idea of followership is gaining momentum as we come to understand that mathematically, there are always going to be fewer leaders than followers (although that same online book site is only up to 390 books on the topic of followership). What if, instead of seeing the act of following as one of weakness, we saw it as a desirable organizational behavior? The apostles certainly thought following was a good idea, and those of us who profess faith do indeed follow God. Ira Chaleff wrote one of the earlier treatises on followership that has stood the test of time—*The Courageous Follower* (1995).

Following: The Companion to Servant Leadership

Chaleff starts by saying that "followers and leaders both orbit around the same purpose; followers do not orbit around the leader." In this sense, both servant leadership and followership can be seen in the most positive viewpoint. Numerous examples are available of leaders who have abused their positions of trust by encouraging their followers to focus only on them rather than organizational purposes. We have only One on whom we should focus—God, our creator, is the only being who should have our complete devotion. In our lives as organizational members, we focus on purpose first of all, and our devotion to God should be that foundational piece that allows us to be remarkable organizational members.

Chaleff offers five guidelines to those who would follow effectively. First, an effective follower accepts responsibility, rather than simply waiting to be told what to do. If there is a need, a follower makes an effort to fulfill it. This isn't permission for anyone in an organization to be overworked. It is simply that a good follower is unlikely to say "It's not my job."

Secondly, the good follower serves the leader, in that the follower helps the leader to conserve energy by taking on tasks as the follower is able. The follower might also serve as a gatekeeper, again, not so that information or people are kept from the leader but that small problems are addressed while they are still small, which is in turn a function of empowerment. An effective follower also defends the leader publicly. This is not from blind obedience but simple loyalty.

Disagreements with the leader are handled privately, not aired publicly.

Coupled with the idea of serving the leader is the third function of a follower, which is challenging the leader. A good follower balances his or her duty to obey (a problematic word at best) with the duty to disobey (similarly problematic). Further, they must be honest with the leader, and confront the leader if abuses arise or if the leader begins to act arrogantly toward his or her followers.

The fourth duty of a follower is to participate in transformation at all levels—transformation of oneself, transformation of the organization and processes, and transformation of the leader. Rather than adhering to a static view of the organization and oneself, a good follower learns and grows alongside the leader.

The final duty of a follower is perhaps the most important. It is their duty to leave the organization when it is time to go. There can be many reasons for leaving. One may be that the follower has grown beyond the challenges of his or her position in the organization and does not have further opportunities. Sometimes people leave because they are exhausted, and staying beyond that point in time would result in inferior service to the organization. Occasionally, good followers leave because they know the group will be able to change direction more easily without them. And sometimes, they leave because of principle. It may be that the values and goals of the organization have changed in a way that the follower no longer feels able to support, or that the follower himself or herself has changed significantly and can no longer ethically claim a place as a member in the organization.

The idea of servant leadership is an important one, and should not be taken lightly or diminished through misuse. Servant leadership and courageous followership form an important partnership in the organization. It is difficult to have one without the other.

Moral Character and Leadership

The threshold of followership is the foundation of character. Enduring character is based on a foundation of moral values. Although there are some who say a person can be moral without having faith, the opposite is not true. A faithful person is a moral one. But what do we mean by morals? Are these the long lists of dos and do nots so common to churches and religious folk? We are talking about a bigger concept, which concerns the collection of behaviors and character traits that a moral leader embraces. According to Michael Josephson, founder of the Josephson Institute, there are six character traits, or pillars of character, that can be found in almost every culture and expression of faith. These are trustworthiness, respect, responsibility, fairness, caring, and citizenship. Let us look at each of these, using the Institutes mnemonics to help us remember them.

Trustworthiness

Think "true blue." This pillar is probably the most complex. It is not so much about trusting others as it is behaving in such a way that others find us worthy of their trust. We must be trustworthy; and, we need to evaluate how and when we are trusting of others (although living a life of suspiciousness can be quite tiring).

Trustworthiness arises from four things. The first is integrity, or living in accordance with positive values. It also means that we are consistent in what we believe, what we say, and what we do. Integrity helps us to avoid intentional harm of others, and gives us the courage to do the right thing even when it is difficult. The second component of trustworthiness is honesty, which is non-negotiable. Dishonesty involves both omission (withholding information) and deception (providing false information). While there are those who say that little white lies to spare another's feelings are important, we have to think about the way we might feel if the situation were reversed. The third aspect of trustworthiness is reliability. We keep our commitments, or as Horton the Elephant said, "I said what I meant, and I meant what I said. An elephant's faithful, 100%." The final component is loyalty, which can be easily misused. People will sometimes ask for loyalty when it is not deserved, to cover up a mistake or something even worse. We do not owe bad behavior to anyone on the basis of loyalty.

Respect

The second pillar of character is respect. This can be remembered by associating it with the color yellow. Think about the golden rule in relationship to this pillar. Respecting others is a different set of behaviors than esteeming others. Respect is something we owe to other human beings as fellow travelers through life. We treat others as we wish to be treated. Respect isn't a means of getting things from others; it is simply the way to behave. Most important, respect, and its companion behavior of listening to others, does not mean we have to agree. We can respectfully disagree with others, but we grant them the same right to hold their opinions and beliefs as we grant to ourselves. We can accept others without expecting them to be like us, and we can respect them without becoming like them.

In addition, the pillar of respect obligates us to adhere to the social manners and conventions of the place in which we find ourselves. While manners may seem like a matter of social etiquette and therefore insignificant, manners are a social necessity that helps us to navigate without running over other people. Essentially, to be respectful is to be mindful that we are all on this planet together. We have no more right to put our needs before others than they do to put their needs before ours.

Responsibility

Responsibility is the third pillar of character. Think of it as a green concept, like being a gardener or financial steward. The main idea behind responsibility is to do one's duty, and to be honorable. We enact responsibility through accountability. We need to face the consequences of our negative behavior or lack of effort. We may not have the power to do a great deal, but we must do what we are capable of doing. In addition, responsibility encompasses self-control, which harkens back to the notion of emotional intelligence. We manage our feelings and impulses in order to act for the common good. In addition, living responsibly propels us toward the pursuit of excellence. Sometimes "good enough" is good enough, BUT, as those made in the image of God we are called to become more like the people we are meant to be. This means rejecting mediocrity and finding ways to grow, not in worldly success or possessions but in knowledge, with our spirituality an expression of that through our work and relationships.

Fairness

The fourth pillar of character is fairness. The Josephson Institute suggests thinking of an orange being divided into equal slices to remember this pillar. The problem is, we are more aware of things that feel unfair than things that feel fair. For example, if things are distributed on the basis of need, it looks quite different from when they are distributed on the basis of merit. To be fair, we need to have consistent criteria for making decisions that are as impartial as possible. The criteria we use for making decisions have to be appropriate to the decision being made. Fairness means following procedures to ensure that our processes are sound. Fairness, when embraced, is linked clearly to justice. Fairness also compels us to be careful about the judgments we make about others. We should not jump to conclusions about them, or share our judgments with others.

Caring

Perhaps the simplest pillar of character to understand is caring. Think of a red heart.

People who act in a caring way are quite different from those who act on the basis of self-interest. Just as respect asks us to cooperate with others in meeting our needs, caring asks that we truly believe that each person matters. Each person's story has significance. A caring person considers how his or her behavior impacts others and acts in ways that do not purposely harm them. Caring is driven by unselfishness and altruism.

Citizenship

The final pillar of character is citizenship, which means understanding that we live in community with others that we must care for. Citizenship can be remembered as purple, for a purple heart in combat. Citizenship requires us to respect authority, not because we are following in blind obedience but because structures allow us to live together with others. We do what we can to help our community, whether it is voting, serving on a committee, picking up trash, etc. And, just as a good follower has the obligation to challenge a leader when necessary, we engage in substantive conflict occasionally, understanding that in both cases there is generally a price to pay for doing so.

We hope you see the relationships among emotional intelligence, servant leadership, courageous followership, and the six pillars of character. They speak to and amplify one another. They call us to rise above self-interest and live in ways that do no harm to others. They call us to do the right thing, even when it's difficult. They call us to be effective leaders as we manage and work with others.

Reflection Five: Leading

Examine the six pillars of character in relationship to your own sense of self. You may want to reference notes you took in class when you were thinking about different impressions of your behavior with respect to specific theories.

In three columns, address these issues:

The specific pillar of character (each pillar will be a row)

Where you stand in relationship behaving this way consistently

10—you have it absolutely nailed

8-9—you can do it pretty consistently

6-7—you're a work in progress

4-5—you understand what you have to do

3 or less—you're not ready to live this way (don't

worry, your grade won't be affected)

The way in which you live out this character trait in the workplace can be beneficial to organizations and/or equip you for success in leadership positions (written in first person, in three sentences).

Adding Leading to your Management Closet

As you build out your closet, use the two facing graph paper pages to accomplish these two tasks.

1. Reflecting on your vocation's inclusion of leadership and followership, consider a process map for your development. What is the process you might engage in to acquire more leadership experiences so that you can specifically develop the pillars of character? Indicate in your process map the intervening followership variables, which you value and will consider in your leadership pursuits and responsibilities.

2. Think of four incredible leaders that you want to emulate and place each of them in a corner of your leadership room. Put a dot in the middle of the page, referencing yourself by identifying three character traits you have which you believe indicate your potential for leadership. Within the "empty space" identify common practices of their leadership, their followership, their character and your own.

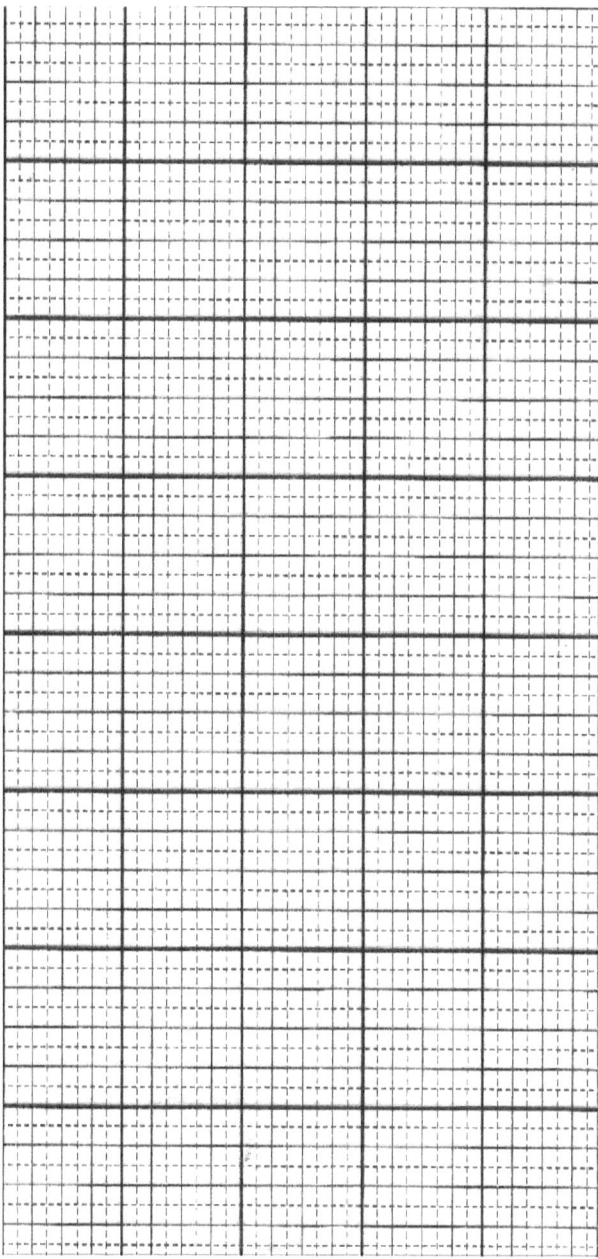

Discussion Takeaways
What did you learn from your peers?

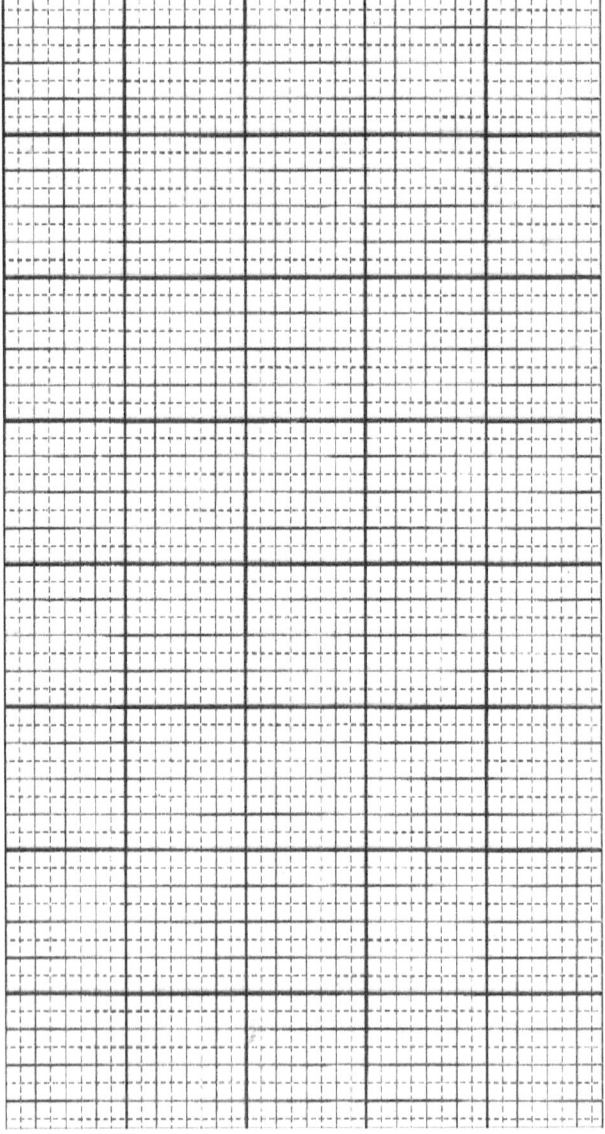

Conclusion

We have come to the end of your course, and this accompanying textbook. You have had much to think about over the last few weeks. As is the case with many things, this ending is only a temporary stop in your journey. You have a chance, before the next semester begins, to take some time to reflect on what you've learned and to make it your own.

Kolb (1984) proposed four stages in active learning, learning that he characterized as creating lasting change in the learner. The cycle of learning can be entered at any stage, but what makes learning last is our commitment to working our way through all the stages.

The most common way people enter the learning cycle is through *concrete experience*. They encounter a significant event or participate in a memorable activity. This can be as simple as a single day or many weeks in a new job. We are triggered to learning, though, because the experience is different in some way from experiences we have had in the past.

We move from concrete experience into *reflective observation*, where we think carefully about our experience, attempting to understand what we did well and what we could have done better. We analyze our own behavior to determine the different things we should repeat in the future, and also to determine those things that ought to be modified.

Connected next to reflective observation is the *abstract conceptualization* stage. The class you have just completed is a long iteration of that particular stage. You've learned many concepts and theories. Many made intuitive sense. Others were more difficult to assimilate into what you already know about your life and how to behave in various situations.

After abstract conceptualization, it's important to think about the way in which you will purposely go about improving your ability to function in new situations. This is the *active experimentation* stage. Theories and concepts are wonderful, but until you actually put them into practice, they don't mean very much.

Now, think back to your first Reflection on vocation. We took you through Kolb's learning cycle. We had you read about vocation (abstract conceptualization). Then we had you think about your experience, reflect on that experience, connect it to the chapter, and commit to some form of action that would increase your understanding of vocation.

In increasing your understanding of management, and your vocation as a manager, it will be helpful to spend some time reflecting on how you will put together the learning you've experienced on vocation as well as on the managerial functions of planning, controlling, organizing, and leading. To that end, we provide you with two last pieces of graph paper, where you may combine aspects of the various pieces you've put into your management closet so far and organize them. Whether or not that organizational structure persists depends on your future experiences and learning around them. Taking the time to reflect and integrate what you have learned now, though, will assist you in future learning.

As you leave, know that our blessings go with you. We hope your life is everything God wants it to be as you follow your vocation. May good health be yours. May you know abundant joy as you walk with God. May you lack for nothing, and may you be generous with what you have. God bless you.

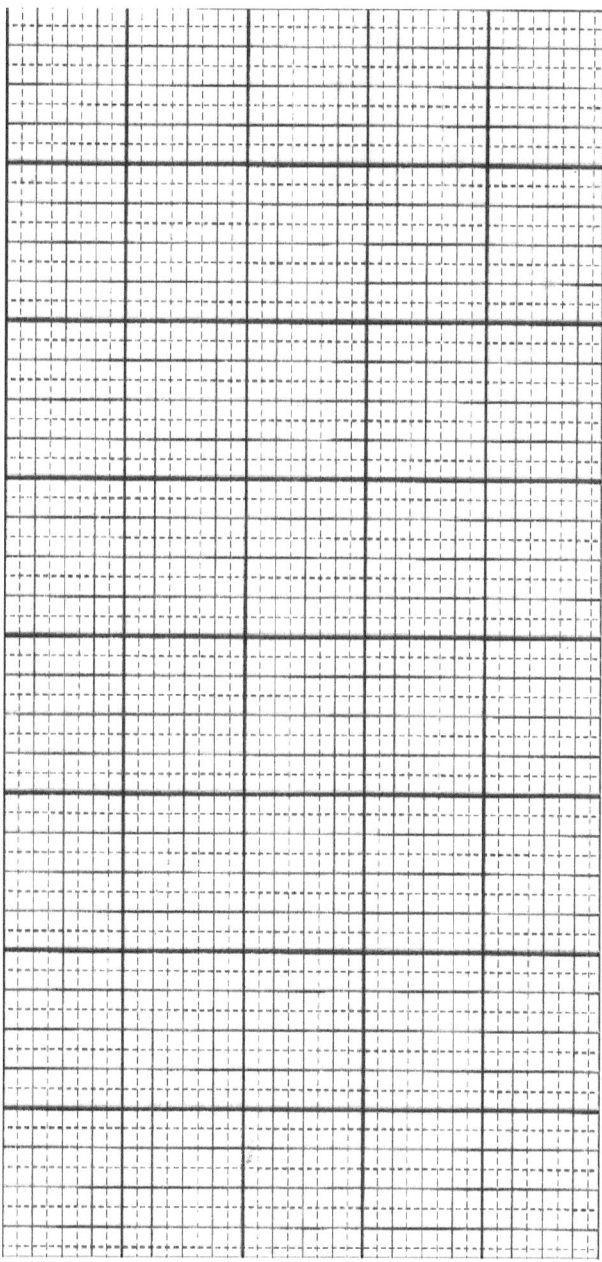

References

Fowler, J. (2000). *Becoming adult, becoming Christian*. San Francisco, CA: Jossey Bass.

Friesen, G. (2004). *Decision making and the will of God* (revised edition). Multnomah Falls, OR: Multnomah Books.

Josephson, M. S. (1996). *Making ethical decisions* (4th ed). Los Angeles, CA: Josephson Institute of Ethics.

Kolb, D. A. (1984). *Experiential learning : Experience as the source of learning and development*. Englewood Cliffs, N.J.: Prentice-Hall.

Maslow, A. (1998). *Toward a psychology of being* (3rd ed.). Hoboken, NJ: Wiley.

Sommers, C. H., & Satel, S. (2006). *One nation under therapy: How the helping culture is eroding self-reliance*. New York: McMillian.

von Rad, G. (2001). *Old Testament theology* (vol. 1). (D. M. G. Stalker, Trans.). Louisville, Kentucky: Westminster John Knox Press Translated by D.M.G. Stalker

Wenham, G. J. (1998). *Genesis 1–15* (vol. 1). Dallas, TX: Word, Incorporated.

About the Authors

Julia J. Underwood (Ph.D., 1998, California School of Professional Psychology) is a professor is the School of Business and Management at Azusa Pacific University, where she has taught since 2001. In addition to her classroom responsibilities, Underwood serves as the Director of Accreditation, Assessment, and Faith Integration for the School of Business and Management. She is active in faculty governance and served as Faculty Moderator presiding over the faculty senate and representing faculty to administration and the Board of Trustees. Additionally, she holds board-level posts with the Christian Business Faculty Association and International Assembly for Collegiate Business Education. Her work with Point Loma Professor Dr. Becky Havens on the dialogical model for faculty to use in creating faith integration experiences in the classroom was the genesis of this book.

Ruth Anna Abigail (Ph.D., 1982, University of Southern California) is professor emeritus at Azusa Pacific University, where she served from 1982 – 2012, first in the department of Communication and last in the College for Adult and Professional Studies. She currently works as a project manager for an aerospace corporation, and her remote assignment allows her to continue her vocation of teaching by offering art classes in her Santa Fe, NM home. In addition to several solo exhibitions as an artist, she is the co-author of *Managing Conflict through Communication*, 5th edition (2013), and *Communication in a Civil Society* (2014). She has also authored many book chapters and convention papers. Her favorite book chapter is "By a Crooked Star: Developing Spirituality in the Context of a Faith-Based Institution, published in *Spirituality in Higher Education*. You can read her occasional blog and see her artwork at www.abigailsmuse.com.